CO$TING
fOR
PROfiT

A PROfESSiONAL's GuidE
TO EffECTivE COSTiNG

By Frances Harder
Author of "Fashion for Profit"

2nd Edition, October 2005

Technical Editor: Evan Smith
Cover Design: Angelena-Simpson Wentzel

Table of Contents

Dedication

I dedicate this important little book, **Costing for Profit**, a sequel to Fashion For Profit to apparel manufacturers who are either in business, or about to begin the exciting and challenging adventure of apparel entrepreneurship. Being inspired and remaining creative while trying to realize a profit can be a daily challenge. I have written this little book with the intent of assisting manufactures to become more profitable in their business. Today's manufacturers represent the future of our industry, and will ultimately be responsible for the economic success of our country's apparel industry. I request that it be a priority for everyone to find ways to support small businesses.

The key people that I would like to thank for helping with the important information needed to compile this book are: Gabriele Goldaper, mentor and long time friend, who has made her career from helping and consulting apparel companies both domestic and internationally. Dana Fried, who has consulted in both startup and multimillion-dollar corporations. Richard Stern for his advice and expertise. Henry Cherner, friend and partner, AIMS (Apparel Information Management System), for his help with content. All have been extremely generous with their advice, positive attitude and expertise in reviewing **Costing for Profit**.

Special thanks to Evan Smith for his help in formatting and assisting with both Fashion For Profit, and Costing for Profit. Also to Jane Mountney Jones for her editing skills and industry expertise.

Fashion For Profit cover girl, and graphic designer; Angelena-Simpson Wentzel who has once again applied her artistic talent to put together the Costing for Profit cover design.

Special thanks to my husband and children.

Preface

Frances Harder, in her words is, the "designer gone insane", who has the apparel industry in her blood! She studied fashion design in England and has enjoyed some exciting design positions in the world of fashion both within the United States, and internationally. She is the daughter of a designer, and the grand daughter of a lace maker from Nottingham, England. Her uncle owned his own clothing manufacturing company in Nottingham, and her aunt had her own dress making business and retail store in Nottingham. Frances's father was a chemist of dye stuff for ICI in Northern England.

Frances has also been an educator and designer for over thirty years, and has taught fashion at many prestigious colleges on both sides of the pond. She was able to call upon all of her talents in founding and developing the Fashion Business Incorporated (FBI), an educational non-profit, which provides business intelligence and business development for small apparel companies. The FBI has become an industry specific model for business development. Commerce is beginning to realize that education is one of the most powerful armaments for their ultimate success. The FBI offers knowledge through seminars and classes, which are drawn from topics that

Frances has conceived. Top consultants have been assembled to teach these classes.

Prior to teaming up with a partner to start the FBI, Frances was an Associate Professor at Otis College of Art in Los Angeles. As a result of her teaching and entrepreneurial experiences, Frances realized that there was a real need for business development information for creative designers, and decided to write a "how to" book Fashion For Profit, which is now in its sixth edition and has become the guide for anyone who wishes to start their own apparel company.

Frances's mantra is "sharing knowledge with others will ultimately benefit us all".

Introduction

Costing For Profit is a comprehensive guide that will help you analyze the preparation of a cost sheet correctly, which will ultimately determine a profitable company. The cost sheet provides critical information for every department involved in the process of producing the finished garment, from design through the production cycle, to distribution of the finished products being shipped to your customer.

The results of proper cost sheet preparation provides a company with essential analytical information for Gross Profit auditing controls. The total of all costs related to the production of the products is called COST OF GOODS SOLD referred to in the industry as COGS.

The cumulative information for all styles will be reflected in your Financial Statement. The difference between the Cost of Goods Sold and the Wholesale Price of the products being offered to the retail market is the Gross Profit.

The percentage between the Cost of Goods Sold and the Wholesale Price reflected in the cumulative sales each season and each year is your profit Margin.

Thus if the Wholesale price of the Garment is $50.00

The Cost of Goods Sold is $25.00

The difference of $25.00 is the Gross Profit

The Gross Profit is 50%.

The gross profit of $25.00 must also provide the funds to pay the company's daily overheads, plus sales representative's commission. This may sound simple but one missed cost or miscalculation can be devastating to your business.

Apparel manufacturers tend to develop or adapt their own way of calculating cost to arrive at their final wholesale price. Some very successful companies have fine-tuned their costing department to make the company profitable. Others unfortunately, unwittingly consider it more important to concentrate on design and realize too late that, although it seems more rewarding to design beautiful clothes. The "Business of Fashion" is a business, and ultimately must be about costing to make a profit.

Because of the many differences used within the industry in calculating their wholesale selling price, I have outlined a number of scenarios in this important little book, which will show a number of ways to calculate your costs to determine your selling price and still realize a profit. Whichever method a company should develop to cost their garments, the end result must result in a profitable margin at the end of the season.

Costing For Profit

Understanding the many components involved in costing a garment correctly will be the key to your company's success.

There are different ways of calculating your wholesale selling price.

Whichever method you choose, your final calculations must result in a profit!

One small miscalculation or a forgotten cost will be devastating to your profit margins, and ultimately undermine the survival of your business.

Small creative companies are often preoccupied with designing, and underestimate the importance of costing and their **actual** overheads.

Their costs are not always correctly detailed until after market, and the orders are in. This can be detrimental to the profitability of a company.

Educate yourself to realize **ALL** cost involved in manufacturing your line and what you will need to operate your business.

Costing For Profit will help you to realize your dream of being a successful designer and the owner of a profitable business.

Why does a dress cost $300 at Riemans and $29.99 at Target?

What contributes to the final selling price of a garment?

- $ Complexity of the design
- $ Status of the label or brand
- $ Produced overseas or domestically
- $ Fabric cost
- $ Retailer store from which the dress is purchased

To the consumer the cost of clothing is often a perceived value

$tep One!

So where do we begin to cost a garment and ultimately realize a profit?

Planning is the key to making your dreams a reality!

1.

Market Research
is Essential

To determine your price bracket or market niche, ask these questions:

$ Who is your target market: age group, social economic income group?

$ What location: statewide, nationwide or global reach?

$ Why would they buy your product?

$ Does your product fill a niche?

$ Is there a need for your product?

$ Which stores would buy your product?

$ Which other brands are your competition?

2.

After Market Research

What would be the selling price range for your product?

$ To cost too high could mean no orders

$ To charge too little could result in no profits, or even worse, losses

$ Miscalculation can be devastating to your profit margins, and could determine whether or not your start-up business can survive

$ Important to retain quality of styling and construction within the set price structure

Informed correct costing will be the key to your company's success

3.

Keep Your Market Analysis Updated

The apparel business is a global industry that is constantly changing. To eliminate risk it is important to have as many facts as possible. Stay on course and consistently monitor your business and THE business as this will influence your costs.

Whether manufacturing domestically or internationally with global distribution, every world variable will have some effect on your costs.

$ Constantly shop stores both locally and globally

$ Check your demographics to make sure it is not changing

$ Don't forget your target market

4.

Formal Business and Financial Plan

$ Make sure that your business plan is updated

$ Has your executive structure changed?

$ How are you financed?

$ Do you have a financial plan for when the BIG orders are written?

$ Plan to grow using the stair steps growth principal - one step at a time. Planning a steady growth will get you there

$ To grow too fast could be a short lived exciting experience

$ Not having time to find the right people to help grow your company could jeopardize your success

A sales rep does not want to write orders if you don't have the funds to deliver!

5.

Branding Process

Creating a brand or logo should be the ultimate goal for any garment manufacturer.

$ The consumer will often pay more for a branded label rather than for a non branded label

$ Eventually licensing a successful brand will create a passive cash flow

$ In other words consumers and other types of product manufacturers will pay you money to advertise your product!!

$ However, you first have to pay out a lot of money to market your own image and brand

$ Advertising requires big bucks, unless you can get on Oprah!!

$ Should you receive free PR or pay for it yourself, make sure you are capable of meeting the demand

$ Have you planned your production capacity and your financing capabilities to match the demand?

It should be noted that for some branded companies there is an optimal level of growth, which they should not exceed. Without the infrastructure in place to deal with rapid growth, it could lead a company to failure.

6.

Trade Mark Licensing

First you must trademark your logo and your company's name

$ It is important to protect your company's image and the integrity of your label

$ If you have a great idea for a new product seek the advice of an expert

$ Trademark licensing should be done by an attorney who understands the apparel industry

$ Are you trade marking your logo in one State or across the US?

$ How will you handle the Global reach?

$ In which other countries do you plan on selling your product?

$ How will you protect your product should you decide to sell internationally?

$ The costs involved in trade marking a brand internationally is very expensive

$tep Two!

Determining Price Point

Your Price Point will usually be determined by your selling price at retail.

7.

Price Range

You must stay within the chosen price range

$ Identify who is your target market & what they will be willing to pay

$ Identify your competition & their price points

$ What is your wholesale and retail price range that your garments should fit into? Then calculate backwards to your costing

$ Make sure that the quality and styling is retained for your market niche

$ Your manufacturing cost + profit. This should calculate to the appropriate profit margin necessary to make a PROFIT!

$ Remember that if your selling price is too high you will cost yourself out of the chosen market

$ If your margins are too low, you are in danger of not making a profit

- **Important to keep in control!**

8.

Cost

COST IS THE ONLY VARIABLE WHICH CAN BE CONTROLLED BY YOU!

$ **Price = Cost + Profit**

$ Understanding the key elements when costing will assure your gross & net profit margin

$ Check your math: Can your garments stand the retailer mark-up of 120% (to them 54% margin) and still have a customer demand for your product? Example:

Your wholesale price: $50.00
Retailer markup (120%): $60.00
Retail selling price: $110.00

Retailer margin: $\frac{60}{110} x100 = 54\%$

$ You must consistently deliver three things:
   $ **Price**
   $ **Quality**
   $ **On-Time Deliveries**

$tep Three!

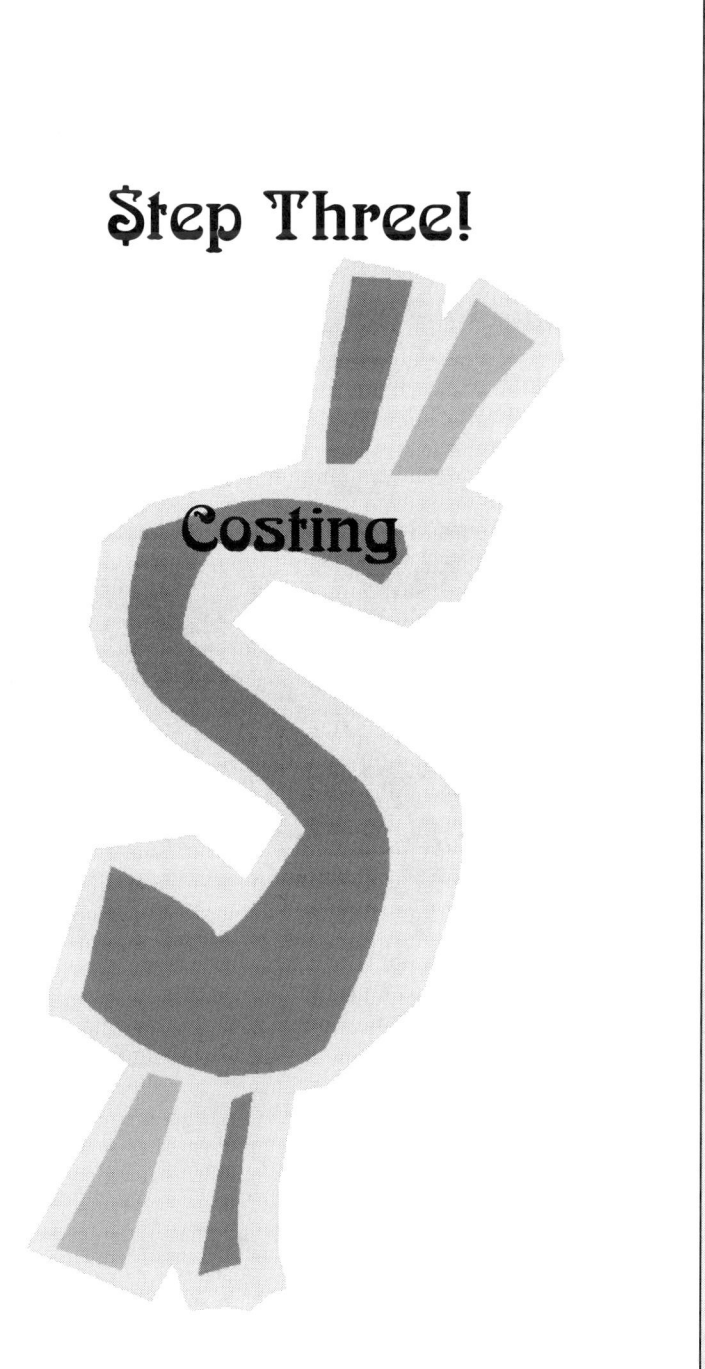

Costing

9.

Three stages of costing:

1. **"Actual cost" of production:** This is the cost to produce the garment and is determined by the fabric, design and production, which can only be reduced by modifying or changing the garment. If producing overseas, this is your landed cost (including freight and duty) or COGS.

2. **Cost plus your markup percentage:** Your mark-up will be determined by a couple of factors: How many units you need to manufacture in order to cover your overhead to realize a profit, and what your market niche will bear. This should be laid out in your business plan and followed.

3. **Retail-selling price:** Having a realistic understanding of the price structure of the market place will help when determining the final cost. Retailers profit margin is usually around a 54% margin.

The final retail price must always be considered when choosing fabric, trims and styling your line. *Don't be tempted to love that fabric from Italy too much without adjusting and simplifying your styling!*

10.

Profit Margin

Your PROFIT MARGIN is PRE-DETERMINED BY YOU & SHOULD NOT BE UNDERCUT

$ If you have a large, potential order from a department store, and they want you to reduce your profit margin, do your math and make sure it is possible to reduce your profit margin and still make a profit

$ Just because you get a large order, it is not necessarily in your company's best interest

$ Take the time to read all sales documents and agreements

$ **You must rework your numbers before you accept orders if there are any requests for discounts!**

$ **If you do receive a large order, check with your contractor to see if they will discount their cost**

$ **However, if you don't get the agreed to orders that your contractor requires for his production run; DON'T TAKE THE ORDER!**

11.

Costs of Ĥandling

Smaller orders from specialty stores require more handling.

$ Results in more hands on time to pick and pack these smaller shipments

$ Increases hourly time needed for workers to complete this process

12.

Importance of Accurate Costing

Underestimating or guessing costs can be disastrous to your long term success.

Incorrect costing can result in losses & eventually bankruptcy for a company.

$ Costing should be done before any orders are written

$ Projecting the size of your production will effect your costing

$ Know your minimum numbers for each style. Don't be tempted to sell ones & twos!!

$ Never guess: Cutting costs, labor costs, trims or yardage!

$ Rework your cost sheets if a style is carried over to a second season

13.

Major Costs

Fabric
Trims
Labor

$ The bigger the order, then unit prices decrease

$ Important to project the amount of goods you need to sell so as to cost realistically. *This is often hard, but **must** be planned for*

$ You may produce domestically, or off-shore; these are major factors in determining the cost of your goods sold

$ If producing off-shore and paying by letters of credit or purchase order financing, be certain to include your financing costs

$ If borrowing money from a lender, asset based financing or using credit cards, you must be certain to include the financing or interest costs

$tep Four!

Cash Flow

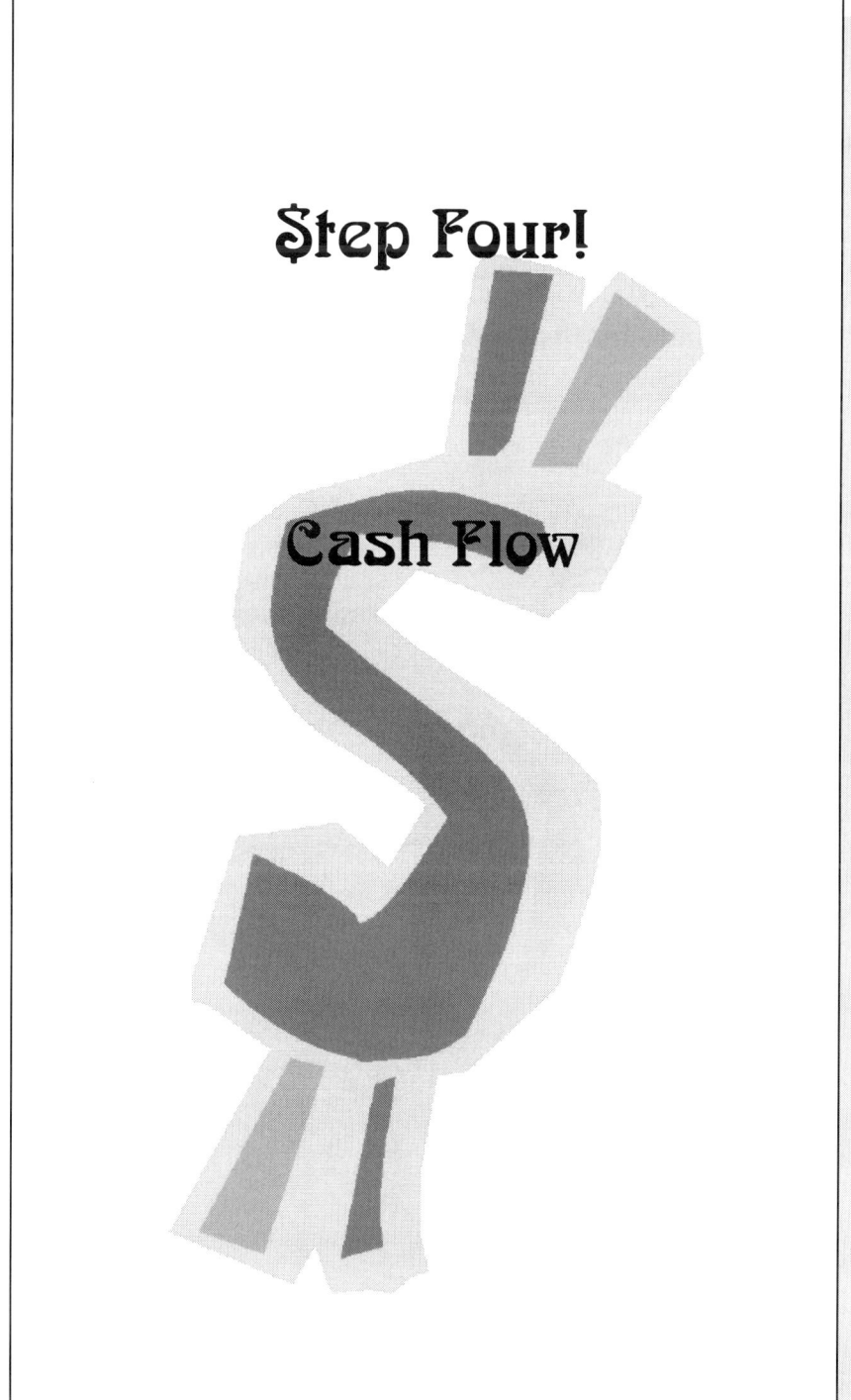

14.

Cash Flow is Key!

Identify potential sources of funding before the need arises.

$ It is critical for you to understand your financial plan and your cash flow needs

$ Turning away orders can be hard, but if the funds are not available to produce your orders you may have no alternative

$ Investigate all funding options before going to market

$ It is most important to plan and retain control of your business!

$ Even with the best of plans, costs are always higher than expected

15.

Working capital has a direct impact on your cash flow

Cash flow is the name of the game for all business owners, a good understanding of working capital is imperative to make any venture successful and profitable.

Know when your invoices are expected to be paid, then you will know when to plan on paying your vendors. However, prepare for late payers.

Try and get your buyers to pay on their credit card. This type of payment is normal practice for small specialty stores. They get the credit card points or mileage and you get paid the day you ship them their goods. This **REALLY** helps your cash flow problems and is a very good reason to stay loyal to your small stores.

Important to note: department stores are a whole different story. You should not sell to them until you are prepared and able to work with them!

Department stores rarely pay on time and they will often charge back to you for reasonable and unreasonable infractions, which they claim you have made.

16.

Building Your Trade Credit

It is important to ask all your vendors, if they will give you time to pay them. It may take a couple of orders before they agree to this, but begin by asking for a 7 days grace period to pay your invoice. As they build trust in your commitment to pay them, ask for more time.

If you get rejected for the full amount, try and bargain with half now and the other half in 10 days.

Even if you don't need the credit in the beginning ask for it anyway. As your company grows, the time will come when you will need that extra time to pay your vendors. The faster your company grows with more orders, the more money you will need to fulfill them.

The credit your vendors extend to you will be built on them taking the financial risk. It will depend on your relationship with them. So be nice!

17.

Seasonal Selling

Saving for a rainy day.

$ It is important to make as much money as possible during the selling months, and calculate your break even financial needs in the off seasons

$ If your sales are not always on the rise, you will need to calculate your monthly overheads to meet the downtime in your sales cycle

$ How many sales do you need to cover overheads? Remember this amount will need to be increased as your sales rise

$ How easy will it be if sales go down to meet the monthly overheads?

18.

Final Selling Price

The final selling price of a garment is a product of total cost of goods sold (If produced overseas, landed cost = finished product, plus freight, plus duty, plus financing cost if using PO, or an LC, plus currency conversion if paying in a foreign currency).

$ Plus the markup needed to reach your desired profit margins

$ Take all this into account, and the retail markup. Does this allow you to sell your product competitively?

19.

Fixed Costs

Fixed Costs are expenses that a business always has. It is important to be aware of them and to keep a track of all fixed costs.

$ Staff – full time and part time

$ Design development - (too often over looked), sample fabric, first patterns, samples, production patterns, quality control, bookkeeping and shipping

$ Overhead costs or fixed costs should not be forgotten, including rent, electricity, payroll etc

$ Keep an eye on these expenses when figuring your markups

$tep Five!

Profit

20.

Examples of Costing

The following will detail different ways to calculate your costs and arrive at a net profit

$ The preferred method: Gross profit less overheads, sales expenses and discounts will give you your true net profit

$ Whichever method you choose to use, the trick is to be aware of all costs and to recost at every level to check for any miscalculations, hidden, or forgotten costs

21.

Keystone Costing

Keystoning is a simplified costing method, which is often used but not always fully understood

$ **Twice your cost, (or is it?)**

$ Are all your overhead expenses calculated or considered into your costing method?

$ Will this really give you a 100% mark-up?

$ **Example:** If your basic cost is $20, you will sell your garment for $40 = **100% mark-up**

$ You go back from the $40 to your cost of $20 , that will equal a **50% gross profit margin**

$ **Important! The gross profit is the foundation to calculate your net profit**

22.

Example of Keystone costs
Without subtracting overhead costs

Fabric Costs

A blouse takes two yards of fabric

2 yards @ $4 .00 per yard	$8.00
Freight for fabric @ 15 cents per yard	$0.30
Total Fabric cost	$8.30

Miscellaneous Costs

Block Fusing	$0.20
7 Buttons @ 2 cents each	$0.14
1 Label@ 2 cents each	$0.02
Miscellaneous costs	$0.36

Labor Charges

Cutting	$1.50
Sewing & Labor	$5.00
Marking & grading	$1.00
Total Labor cost	$7.50

Your Total cost	**$16.16**
Keystone: 100% Mark-up	**$16.16**
Total Wholesale Price	**$32.32**

(You may round out your wholesale price)

23.

Keystone Gross Profit
Without subtracting Overhead costs

$ Keystone: 100% mark-up $16.16

$ Total wholesale price $32.32

$ 100% markup = 50% gross profit

$ This calculation does not consider your overhead expenses including: rent, administrative and sales expenses

$ These must be deducted from your gross profit to get to your net profit

Important: Smaller manufacturers should aim for at least a 55% to 65% gross profit margin, because of the small amount of units manufactured.

24.

Net Profit Cost Calculations
Without subtracting overhead cost

Wholesale Price	$32.32
Subtract Cost of Goods Sold (COGS)	$16.16
Gross Profit	$16.16

Net Profit Calculation

Wholesale Price	
Your selling price	$32.32
Subtract Sales commission 10%	$3.23
After commission	$29.09
Subtract Actual Cost of Garment	$16.16
Net Profit **Total**	$12.93
without subtracting overheads	

Net Profit is your tax base

25.

Net Profit Margin Calculations
Without subtracting overheads

Divide the Net Profit by the wholesale price, then multiply by 100

$$\frac{\$12.93}{\$32.32} \, x100 = 40\%$$

40% is your Net Profit Margin

(Without including overheads or discounts allowable)

26.

Discounts Allowable for Early Payments

Buyers will often ask for a discount on their orders if they agree to make payment to you within 30 days

$ Discounts vary but normally fall into the 8% to 10%

$ Even if they don't intend to pay within 30 days they will often expect these discounts

$ It can take between 60 to 90 days to receive payment from major department stores

$ This should be carefully monitored as it will affect your cash flow

27.

Net Profit Cost Calculations
With discounts included but no overhead costs

Wholesale Price	$32.32
Subtract Cost of Goods Sold (COGS)	$16.16
Gross Profit margin	**$16.16**

Net Profit Calculation

Wholesale Price	$32.32
Subtract Discounts allowable 10%	$3.23
Your new selling price	**$29.09**
Subtract Sales commission 10%	$2.90
After discounts and commission	$26.19
Subtract Actual Cost of Garment	$16.16
Net Profit **Total**	**$10.03**

without including overhead costs

Net Profit is your taxable base

28.

Net Profit Margin Calculations
With discounts included but no overhead costs

Divide the Net Profit by the wholesale price, then multiply by 100

$$\frac{\$10.03}{\$32.32}\, x100 = 31\%$$

**31% is your Net Profit Margin
(Without overhead costs)**

29.

Should You Add Overheads in Your Costs?

Is it important to list ALL expenses in a cost sheet?

$ Often, this method can cost a company out of the market, as the final selling cost will calculate too high!

$ **However, it is interesting to compare the different methods – so we will show you!**

$ In calculating your gross profit margin, do not include any expenses that are not directly related to the cost of the finished goods

$ Overhead costs are not usually included in gross profit margin calculations

$ If you include your overhead costs in your cost sheet, they should be calculated on the number of units you plan on selling

30.

Example of Keystone costs
Including overhead

Fabric Costs

A blouse takes two yards of fabric	
2 yards @ $4 .00 per yard	$8.00
Freight for fabric @ 15 cents per yard	$0.30
Total Fabric cost	$8.30

Miscellaneous Costs

Block Fusing	$0.20
7 Buttons @ 2 cents each	$0.14
1 Label@ 2 cents each	$0.02
Miscellaneous costs	$0.36

Labor Charges

Cutting	$1.50
Sewing & Labor	$5.00
Marking & grading	$1.00
Total Labor cost	$7.50

Overhead (Calculated on units produced)

	$1.50
Your Total cost	$17.66
Keystone: 100% Mark-up	$17.66
Total Wholesale Price	$35.32

(You may round out your wholesale price)

31.

Keystone Gross Profit Calculations
Including overheads

Keystone: 100% mark-up $17.66

Total wholesale price $35.32

100% markup = 50% gross profit

This calculation considers your overhead expenses: Administration, rent, cars...

32.

Net Profit Calculations
Including overheads & discounts

Wholesale Price	$35.32
Subtract Cost of Goods Sold (COGS)	$17.66
Gross Profit margin	$17.66

Net Profit Calculation

Wholesale Price	$35.32
Subtract Discounts allowable 10%	$3.53
Your new selling price	**$31.79**
Subtract Sales commission 10%	$3.18
After commission is paid	$28.61
Subtract Actual Cost of Garment	$17.66
Net Profit **Total**	**$10.95**

Net Profit is your taxable base

33.

Net Profit Margin
Including Overheads & Discounts

Divide the Net Profit by the wholesale selling price and then multiply by 100

$$\frac{\$10.95}{\$35.32} x100 = 31\%$$

31% is your Net Profit Margin

34.

Profit Comparisons
With or without Overheads

Whichever costing method you choose, the bottom line will be the real profit your company will ultimately take to the bank

A profit can only be realized when you fully understand the total components that need to be considered when calculating your net profit margin.

$tep $ix!

Mass Production

35.

Mass Production

"Mass" produced clothing can allow for a smaller mark-up due to the large quantities produced at one time.

For the most part mass produced clothing is produced off-shore.

Because of the lower cost of off-shore workers wages, it is difficult for US manufacturers to remain competitive.

Domestic contractors normally work with a 30% profit margin.

36.

Off-Shore Production

Deciding to produce your goods off-shore will affect your wholesale selling price. However, before venturing abroad it is very important to answer these questions to fully understand the advantages and the disadvantages of taking this route.

$ The question is why go off-shore?

$ What can off-shore versus domestic production offer?

$ When first thinking of taking production off-shore it will be important to test the system, and not put all your eggs into one basket

$ Begin with a 80/20 split. Diversify your production.

$ Keep 80% here, and test with 20% for first time off-shore production

$ Where do you go to find the right reliable resources?

$ How will your quality control be monitored?

$ Will you need to find an agent to represent your company and check your production?

$ How will you obtain lines of credit?

$ What is a Letter of Credit and how much will it cost?

\$ How much Duty will there be on your imported goods, and how much will you pay? Duties vary depending on where the goods are produced

\$ How will Quotas effect my production off shore?

\$ How will currency charges and conversions costs add to your costs?

\$ Will you still be able to meet delivery dates?

\$ How much extra time will you need to allow for off-shore production?

\$ How much should you allow for shipping costs?

These are reasons why many smaller companies produce only domestically where they can better control their quality, production and delivery times.

37.

Know Your Timelines

If you are investigating off-shore sourcing it will be important to understand the lead time. If your production is domestic and you are in the contemporary market then timing will be everything. Look at your delivery timeframe and know where your offshore production cycle is at all times.

Once you find an off-shore source, what happens next?

- $ Do they need to purchase supplies, or do they already have them?
- $ Do they make the goods, or have to send somewhere else?
- $ How do they deal with their sub contractors?

It is very important to understand how long it's going to take to get the goods here and where they are at all times; from fabrication to production, to shipping.

It's a big mistake to underestimate the time line. If your shipment is late this will result in more dilution and cancelled orders.

38.

Letters of Credit

$ It will be important to get a full understanding of how to open letters of credit

$ Talk with your bank and your factor. Some Asian companies will give credit much sooner than they used to

$ As with all aspects of running a successful business, it will be important to build reliable relationships

$tep $even!

Custom Made Clothing

&

Couture Costing

39.

Custom Made Clothing
&
Couture Costing

When costing a couture garment it is important to establish an hourly rate for the creator of these one of a kind garments.

One of a kind, couture, or sometimes referred to as wearable art, has nothing in common with manufactured clothing, as the costing must be calculated by the hours of work entailed in creating **one** finished garment.

If the custom-made piece has been commissioned, ask for a fifty percent up-front deposit and the other half on completion.

To guarantee payment upon completion, finished pieces may be shipped either COD cashiers check, or pro forma. (COD should only be agreed to with established vendors).

Important to have in writing and signed by your customer before commencing work, that any changes made to the design by your customer will incur an extra charge.

$tep Eight!

Private Label

40.

Private Label

If commissioned to manufacture for a private label or for a branded logo, or for any special orders with embroidery, (example to manufacturer for Disney) it is important to require a 50% deposit up front. The remaining 50% is payable upon completion.

The reason for this requirement is that it would be impossible to sell the branded product should you not get paid and are left with the product.

If commissioned to manufacturer private label for a specialty store your payment would be invoiced using the normal method.

$tep Nine!

Preparing a Cost Sheet

41.

Filling in a Cost Sheet

Filling in the cost sheets yourself will be an invaluable lesson, and will teach you the true meaning of costing.

There will be times that an adjustment will need to be made to the final gross margins to keep garments in the correct price range.

$ Only you can make this important decision!

$ Can the selling price be lowered?

Be certain you can afford to adjust your wholesale selling price DOWN!

42.

The following should be included or considered into a cost sheet

$ Date

$ Style number and design number (name if applicable)

$ Fabric mill – Cost per yard

$ Fabric yields, (include fabric shipping costs)

$ Linings

$ Trim cost, including fusing

$ Cutting

$ Labor & sewing

$ Swatch of the fabrics, trims

$ Send out information e.g. fusing, pleating, embroidery, printing etc

$ Packaging

$ Mark-up percentage: Which should consider: *Overhead costs, fixed costs, operational costs, sales Representative percentage, tradeshow expenses, chargebacks. discounts or markdowns must by taken into account when calculation your final mark-up percentage, (not forgotten when selling to department stores)*

$ Wholesale price

$ Gross profit calculations

$ Net profit calculations

3.

Calculate Your Fixed Cost

Office staff salaries – More economic to employ part-time staff or hourly paid workers.

Full time salaries with benefits can add another 30 cents per hour on the dollar paid.

$ Rent – Contract out as much as possible in order to keep your overheads down and your office space rental as low as possible

$ Utilities etc

$ Lease rather than buy. Monthly payments may be easier to figure into accounting rather than a large cash outlay if there is a cash crunch

A realistic percentage for fixed overheads should be around 5% - 7% of wholesale price. If you have a 30% gross profit margin, and your fixed expenses are 10% of your net sales, this will undermine your profit. If that is the case, try to reduce your fixed expenses.

44.

Operational Costs

Product development – is an operational cost but only when developing new designs.

Design departments should be monitored closely for excessive expenditure:

How many samples produced per season?

The average cost to develop one sample is approximately $500; fabric, first patterns, cutting, sewing, fitting and adjusting...

Use computer programs to render your first designs. Scan your fabrics then drape virtually for your design development and for finished styles.

45.

Variable Costs

Actual costs of product

$ Fabric

$ Trims

$ Labor

$ Size of cuts

Agreeing to produce smaller lots can be costly and erode your profits.

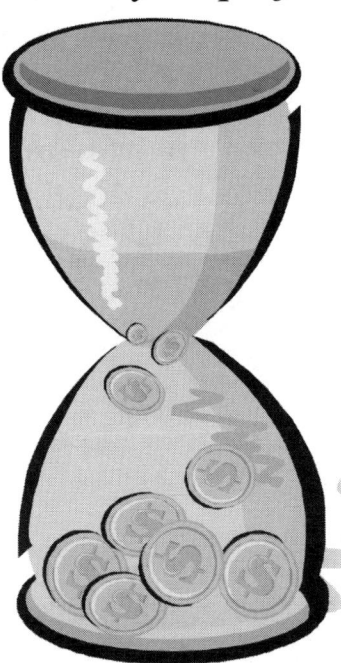

46.

Sales Representatives Percentages, Expenses and Discounts

The percentage allowed your sales representative for sales commission plus showroom and tradeshow expenses should be considered into your costs.

$ Also - Terms of Sales influencing the cost. Discounts for prompt payment by the store are often asked for by the buyers

$ Calculate the percentage of allowable discounts you can afford

$ The commission paid to your sales representatives is based on the final agreed to selling price (after allowable discounts) and the actual units shipped to the store

$ Showroom participation fees and trade show expenses should also be considered, as these can be very costly

$ *Better to pay a higher percentage to your sales rep than pay a fixed monthly showroom participation fee*

$tep Ten!

Chargebacks

47.

Chargebacks Destroy Your Profits

Chargebacks undermine your gross profits and should be carefully monitored. Keep a close watch in the areas where they are most prevalent:

$ Is it a problem with shipping, labeling, hangers, packaging or out of specifications?

$ Is it quality control, damages, or are there sizing issues?

$ Is it late shipments?

$ If you are selling to department stores it is usual to add between 12% and 15% to the cost sheet for the inevitable discounts and charge-backs. If you sell to specialty stores, the percentage should be around 6 to 8 percent

48.

Other Chargeback & Markdown Costs from Major Department Stores

$ Too few garments selling at full price – Retailer makes you share in the losses from discounted sales

$ Charges for advertising or promoting the product in store flyers and newspaper advertisements

$ Department stores will charge larger manufacturers rent to have their line displayed in a high traffic area within the store

Remember! Markdown money or store credit adds to the manufacturer's variable costs.

49.

Dilution of Profit

This is the difference between what you invoice the retailer (customer) and what you get paid from your customer.

Example:

$ Non-paying customers

$ Chargeback

$ Returns

$ Store discounts

$ Late shipment

$ Damaged goods

$ Purchase order (P.O.) violations

Generally the more expensive the product, the higher the percentage of dilution of sales. Customer returns are higher because of the pricing structure and should be an added cost consideration.

50.

Shipping Dates

$ It is better to ship at the beginning of the shipping window

$ This will allow for reorders and your goods to get onto the store floor for a longer period of time, which means they have a longer sell through time

$ Shipping at the end of your delivery window means that the goods aren't on the floor for that long, and they may be marked down sooner because of new goods arriving

$ Make sure that all separates are shipped together, (matching tops to bottoms)

$ Should your production not go as planned and you have a problem with related separates which you cannot ship together, then contact the buyer and inform them of any delivery problems

It is crucial to control all parts of your production.

51.

Retailer's Mark-up

Retailers buy your product at a wholesale price, then add their overhead costs plus profits: between 100% to 125% to get the retail selling price.

$ Retailers normally pay for any shipping charges

$ They will have requirements as to the shipping instructions and packaging details. It is important to understand your exact responsibilities for shipments and any hidden costs?

$ Anticipate your customer's demands and include them when considering your costs!

$ Do not let the retailers dictate their price, unless you know your profit margin can bear their asking price. It is important to protect your profit margin, and stay in control of your product costs

$ Ask your sales reps NOT to agree to store discounts without your approval

52.

Retailers Selling Price

It is important to establish a suggested retail selling price with your retailers.

If a retailer decides to mark up too high your line may not sell.

Your sales rep and/or yourself should inquire weekly with your accounts as to how your line is **"selling through"**.

This will provide you with important information as to which designs are selling, and which are your best sellers.

The best selling items can be carried over to your next season's line.

The styles that are not selling should be analyzed as to the problem: fabric, fit, styling, or maybe you where ahead of the game with trend forecasting?

$tep Eleven!

Recosting

53.

Importance of Recosting

Recost every new style, for every new season, and remember to rework the cost sheet.

$ Beware of using the same cost sheet when changing fabrication, even if using the same style

$ There could be hidden costs that you are unaware of when changing the fabrication, such as differences in the fabric cost, the fabric width, the marker, production, finishing, pressing, etc

54.

Financing Your Line

Depending on your funding it may be wise to start with small orders that you can self finance so that when mistakes are made it will not be too financially and emotionally devastating to the company.

$ You will learn by your mistakes

$ The secret to costing and financial success is understanding how to plan your companies growth

$ Finding financing for large orders when just starting a company will be difficult unless you have:

> ¢ Your own savings

> ¢ Family or friends as investors

> ¢ Line of credit

> ¢ Collateral

Don't use credit cards, the interest rates are too high!

55.

Factoring Orders or Using your assets to grow your business

It is nearly impossible to factor a new business without a proven track record.

$ A company needs to show experience and a profit

$ It is very difficult to get a 1st line of credit from traditional factoring

$ A company will need at least $500,000 in annual orders before a factor (first line of credit) or refactor (second line of credit) will agree to loan you money against your receivables

$ It helps to have orders from reputable stores

$ Begin early to build relationships with factors

$ Remember, factors take the risk and so they have to be cautious with their money

$ **You must retain a good credit rating!**

56.

how a Factor Can help your Business

$ A factor will advance funds against your receivables (written orders) or against your collateral

$ Why factor? A factor can assist your company with cash flow problems and help solve financial burden

$ The day you ship you will receive 70% to 80% of invoice orders. You pay interest to the factor, (usually 2% above prime), plus a fee, until the invoice is paid by the store to the factor

$ Factors also check stores credit plus take the financial risk

$ They collect the money owed and then pay you the other 20% to 30% less fees

57.

Purchase Order Financing

Is it a financial liability or a financial asset to your company?

P.O. financing can be risky and therefore you must understand how to make it work for your company's cash flow crunch.

Money is loaned against your written orders to help with your up front production costs; fabric, sewing, etc.

However, it is a very expensive way to borrow money and you must calculate this into your costs.

You will be borrowing and paying interest on the loan for at least two to three months before you are able to repay.

Can you afford this type of loan? It is important to factor the fees plus interest into your costs.

58.

Understand Delivery Dates

Many design driven companies become enamored of their own designs and are convinced that the market will fall in love with their product. They often stock up without any regard to orders or to the financial downside. The goods inevitably end up discounted and consequently, there will be heavy losses to account.

Caution is advised when speculating sales and asking for any kind of financial backing.

$ You should be 80% sold before arranging for any financing

$ **Not 20% and speculating 80%!**

$ This will result in inventory build up

Important to build inventory on orders written, not on speculation! Management of inventory is key!

59.

Understand Delivery Dates

Late deliveries will result in cancelled orders or chargebacks, so it is important to know your delivery dates, which will reflect on your production dates.

$ If March 30th, April 30th and May 30th are delivery dates, then you must work out your production dates with your contractor to avoid missing shipping deadlines

$ Get delivery dates in a written contract with your contractor

Stick to your drop dead dates!

$tep Twelve!

Garment Costing for Success

10 Point Checklist for Profitable Results

60.

1. Development Cost

Whatever type of garment you manufacture there is always development. These are known as hidden costs and should not be ignored.

Design room, sample room & product development cost can be top heavy. It is very important to control these cost as they are too often over looked.

Track these expenses by the season; number of samples produced, amount of sample yardage, and how many times a sample is made before it is accepted in the line.

2. First Sample or Prototype Cost

Check the number of times the average sample is made before the final garment is approved.

Samples produced should be controlled. Contractors charge approximately three times the cost of final production cost for sampling.

Typically a design driven contemporary company is higher-end and should cost for higher margins. However, they also tend to design and sample far too many, which results in too many SKU's.

Utilize computer software programs to help with product development costs, fabric rendering for color and style choices.

The average cost of one sample is around $500 to develop the pattern, fabric, cut, sew, fit, and cost.

3. Fabric Cost for Sampling

Fabric used for samples can add up. Keep a record of this part of development. You may be surprised at the amount of sample yardage ordered and not used.

All those beautiful Italian fabrics at textile shows can often be too tempting for creative designers!

4. Pattern Development Costs

Experienced patternmakers can save a manufacturer money. Make sure you pay them for their experience, it will save you money in the long run!

Pattern making can be more costly than realized. Keep an account of this part of your business expenses.

5. Yield of Fabric Costs

Your fabric expense may be 40% to 50% of the direct cost of the garment. Making sure that you are not wasting fabric and that your markers are good and tight is going to affect the overall profitability of your business.

Employing an experienced production person could save on overall expenses in the long term

6. Trim Costs and Findings

Forgetting to include trims into a cost sheet will result in erosion of profits

Whether it's zippers, labels, fusing, embroidery, elastic or other trims, make sure you are aware of the correct amount each garment needs. Haste makes waste and will take away your direct profit.

7. Contracting or Labor Costs

Sewing is another part of the garment cost that is usually 30% to 40% and should be fixed early in determining the cost of a garment.

Work only with reliable and legal contractors who can produce your goods on time.

Note for California and New York apparel manufacturers *– For your own records keep a copy of your contractors contracting license. Working with illegal contractors could result in confiscation of your goods, which could result in late deliveries or in some cases loss of a season. The contractor will also ask to see your manufacturing license and take a copy for their own records.*

8. The Cost of Cutting

Before cutting can begin make sure the fabric is checked on arrival for flaws and for width variations.

If you find irregularities with your fabrics Chargeback the mills as soon as possible. Timing is important.

Once you cut into the fabric, it is yours!

In-house cutting is often preferred to keep a check on waste.

Do not allow a build-up of aging fabric inventory.

9. Production Overheads

Real estate prices, electric costs, phone costs, accounting, transportation, quality control, shipping and packaging, even hangers and plastic bags are important expenses that should not be ignored.

10. Quality & Inventory Control

Quality control of the first production sample and production itself must have continuity otherwise there will be returns.

Important to make production samples for your contractor.

Returns equal reduction of your profits.

Inventory Control: Don't keep stock for more than a season. The longer you hang on to inventory the less it is worth.

61.

Items Influencing Garment Cost

If the garment cost is too high then you must review the situation and find a solution to reducing the costs:

$ Simplification of styling

$ Fabric yield

$ Total number of pattern pieces

$ Total number of notches

$ Total number of steps involved in the garment construction

$ Seam finishes, pressing, fusing, etc

If simplification cannot be achieved…

DROP IT FROM THE LINE!!

62.

Cost of Fabric

Consider buying directly from the mill (a problem for small companies, due to large minimums).

Can you afford a fabric rep?

Fabric shipping costs?

Number of yards per garment?

Ease of handling, silk, velvet, matching plaids, stretch, spreading needs, shrinkage under steam iron, pre-shrinking, etc.

Color variation, dye lots, garment dye, problems of fading in the store window, washing instructions, etc. It is important to test your own care labels. Swimwear manufacturers have to test garments for chloride and salt damage.

Size of the cutting tickets or the units to be cut will also affect the final cost of the garment

63.

Contracting Out Work

Contracting work out to reliable contractors will allow you to keep your overhead expenses down. Some of the services you can contract:

$ In-house, or outside sewing contractor

$ Grading & marker maker service

$ Cutting service

$ Inspection of finished goods

$ Picking and packaging orders

$ Shipping services

$ Accounting services

$ Payroll services

$ Domestic Production

$ Off-Shore Sourcing

It is important to have references for any of the above contractors.

64.

Construction Costs

$ Larger lots (contractors' costs go down when you have 300 garments or more)

$ Smaller businesses usually have to shop for contractors who specialize in smaller lots, which will increase unit cost

$ Grading and marking costs are computed on the number of the pattern pieces in one style

65.

Quality of Design

More complicated designs can be seen in "Better" priced clothing, along with more expensive quality fabrics, trims, linings, fusing and construction of garment.

A better fit and quality of garment should be evident in the higher-price range.

Details of better fitting garment can be evident in more seams, darts, inner construction and linings. Bigger seam allowances and hems equal more fabric usage, which in turn equals a more expensive garment.

Examples of some seams: French, flat felled, slot, topstitching, corded seams, open welt seams, more stitches per inch etc.

$tep Thirteen!

Four Levels of Costing Methods

66.

Finally consider those four important costing methods

Level 1 - Quickie Costing

Design department costing for the first sample

$ Estimate cost of each style before they are produced

$ Don't waste time and money to sample if they are obviously going to cost you out of your market niche

$ Quickie costing can be applied after a sample has been made and before they are added to the line

$ Pull the style before it gets into the line and will become a financial looser

67.

Level 2 - Costing for Sales

Critical costing that must be exact

Management, Production, Design & Sales Dept. should all agree to your selling price.

$ This is where you set your selling price

$ You cannot change your wholesale price once it is set

$ All materials, cutting and contracting costs must be thoroughly understood and included

68.

Level 3 - Production Costing

Double check to see if your actual costs are correct. They should not be off by more than 3% to 5%.

This is where most problems can be found.

If costing is off you must cull the style.

If sales have been made, call buyer and tell them you have to pull the style but you have a **better** selling style for them. Never tell them you have made a mistake!

Important to cut your losses when you know something is not working!

69.

Level 4 - Account Dept. Costing

This is done at the end of the season to calculate average mark-up on all the garments sold and to track returns plus chargebacks.

Count every invoice and divide by sales, this will give you your season's average mark-up. Even better to do it by styles.

Accounting costing is done to help you to project sales and to understand how much cash flow you will need.

Lastly, the results of each style in either the line, or the collection provide historical information that will be important for both the following season and for the same season next year.

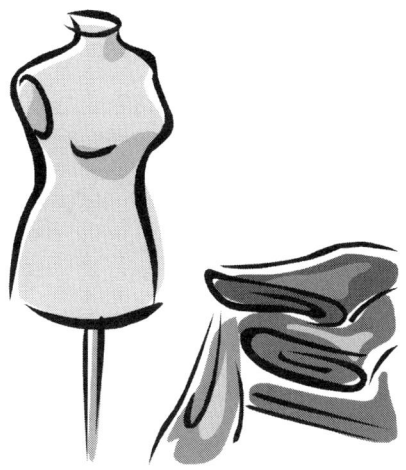

70.

Remember 80% of your business will be in 20% of your styles

$tep Fourteen!

Computer Software Needs

71.

Computer Software Programs to Calculate Your Costs and Help with Production Needs

Once data is entered into one of the many apparel specific software programs an accurate costing is calculated for each style produced.

$ Yardage cost

$ Labor costs

$ Fixed costs

$ Operational costs

$ These programs will calculate the gross profit margin and the net profit margins

Important to remember, the computer is a tool and is only as good as the user, so be sure that the information programmed into the computer is correct! Check more than one software program to find the one which will suit your needs.

In Conclusion

Your wholesale price will often have nothing to do with the customers' perceived value of the garment. It relates to the final selling price, or the niche market that you have so carefully decided to fill.

Stay focused on your niche, control ALL your costs, and consistently monitor your business.

Listen to your customers' needs and your management team.

Find the right team to work with who understands the apparel business today! Even if you have to pay more to get the right people it will pay off in the long run.

It is important for a design driven company to find a good CPA who understands the apparel industry, and who can do your quarterly reports. Your factor will ask to see these reports and will use them to monitor how your company is running. Design and sales alone will not make a successful company. YOU NEED A GOOD CFO who will track your internal operations and your inventory to your sales.

Remember! It is not only about creating beautiful clothes, it is about running a profitable business; a commercial venture, from which you must realize a profit in order to stay in business.

Appendices

Apparel Acronyms

ASN	ADVANCED SHIPPING NOTICE
BOM	BILL OF MATERIAL
C & F	COST AND FREIGHT
CAB	COMPUTER AIDED BUSINESS
CAD	CASH AGAINST DOCUMENTS
CAD	COMPUTER AIDED DESIGN
CAFTA	CENTRAL AMERICAN FREE TRADE AGREEMENT
CAM	COMPUTER AIDED MANUFACTURE
CFR	COST & FREIGHT
CFTA	CANADA FREE TRADE AGREEMENT
CIA	CASH IN ADVANCE
CIF	COST, INSURANCE, FREIGHT
CIM	COMPUTER INTEGRATED MANUFACTURING
CIT	COURT OF INTERNATIONAL TRADE
COD	CASH ON DELIVERY
COGS	COST OF GOODS SOLD
CPO	CUSTOMER PURCHASE ORDER
DBA	DOING BUSINESS AS
DLSE	DIVISION OF LABOR STANDARDS ENFORCEMENT
DOC	DEPARTMENT OF COMMERCE
DOS	DATA OPERATING SYSTEM
EDI	ELECTRONIC DATA INTERCHANGE
EOM	END OF MONTH
FOB	FREE ON BOARD
FTC	FEDERAL TRADE COMMISSION
GUI	GRAPHICS USER INTERFACE
ITC	INTERNATIONAL TRADE COMMISSION
JPG	JPEG (Joint Photographic Experts Group)

L/C	LETTER OF CREDIT
LDP	LANDED-DUTY-PAID
NAFTA	NORTH AMERICAN FREE TRADE AGREEMENT
NRF	NATIONAL RETAIL FEDERATION
OTB	OPEN TO BUY
OTS	OPEN TO SELL
PDF	PORTABLE DOCUMENT FORMAT
PDS	PATTERN DESIGN SYSTEM
PO	PURCHASE ORDER
PFD	PREPARE FOR DYE
RFID	RADIO FREQUENCY IDENTIFICATION
RN#	REGISTERED NUMBER
ROI	RETURN OF INVESTMENT
SKU	STOCK KEEPING UNIT
UCC	UNIFORMED CODE COUNCIL
UOM	UNIT OF MEASURE
UPC	UNIVERSAL PRODUCT CODE
UPS	UNITED PARCEL SERVICE
VAT	VALUE ADDED TAX
VPO	VENDOR PURCHASE ORDER
WIP	WORK IN PROCESS
WTO	WORLD TRADE ORGANIZATION

Fashion Business Incorporated
About the Fashion Business Inc.

Frances Harder founded the Fashion Business Inc. in 1999 with one goal in mind: to provide much needed business intelligence and training to start up, fledgling, and fast growing apparel manufacturers within the Los Angeles fashion industry. Since its inception, the FBI has gained a 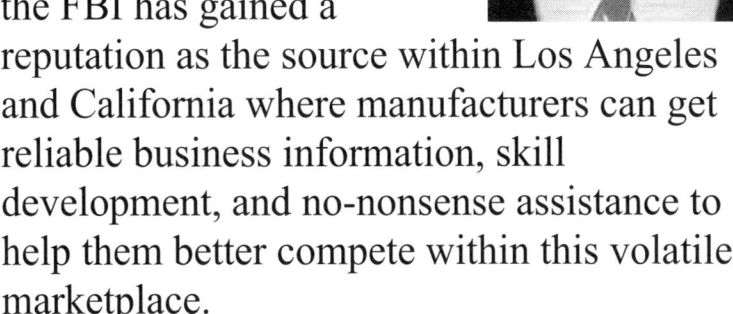 reputation as the source within Los Angeles and California where manufacturers can get reliable business information, skill development, and no-nonsense assistance to help them better compete within this volatile marketplace.

Through its training and informational seminars, the FBI has worked with more than 3,000 existing and start up companies, providing business owners critical information regarding such topics as: Compliance and Monitoring Sub-Contractors, Costing for Profit, EDI (Electronic Data Interchange), as well as long term training that cover the gamut for people exploring the feasibility of starting apparel companies, to strategic planning, geared toward manufacturers who are ready to grow their companies to the next level. Though the FBI encourages companies to become part of the organization's membership by giving discounts for services, all educational programs are open to the general public.

The FBI is a highly focused, educational non-profit (501(c)3), making it ideally suited to help the owners of local apparel manufacturers to gain the knowledge they need in order for their businesses to not only survive, but to prosper.

The FBI's new Business Resource training facility in downtown Los Angeles is in the heart of the Los Angeles Fashion District. This state of the art 5,000 square foot center operates in donated space located in the prestigious New Mart. The center was built with the help of a generous grant from the City of Los Angeles Department of Water and Power Economic Development

Department. The new center houses a cooperative showroom, computer lab, photo studio, classroom space and general office space. The center serves as a one-stop-shop for services and resources for FBI members as well as for the general public.

The center is staffed with industry professionals and seminars and training classes are taught by an impressive list of experienced consultants who are available to provide counseling on a broad range of topics, and at various levels of complexity and sophistication.

The FBI's business model of providing business intelligence and practical training to apparel manufacturers has garnered a great deal of interest from other cities around the country that have significant apparel sectors. The FBI has now partnered with two other business centers, which will increase FBI membership and provide FBI's business intelligence to San Diego and to San Francisco. Seattle is also in the process of partnering with the FBI.

FBI Membership Information:

Annual Business Membership: $200.00

Out of State membership: $150.00

Student membership: $35.00

Industry Partner: $750.00

www.Fashionbizinc.org

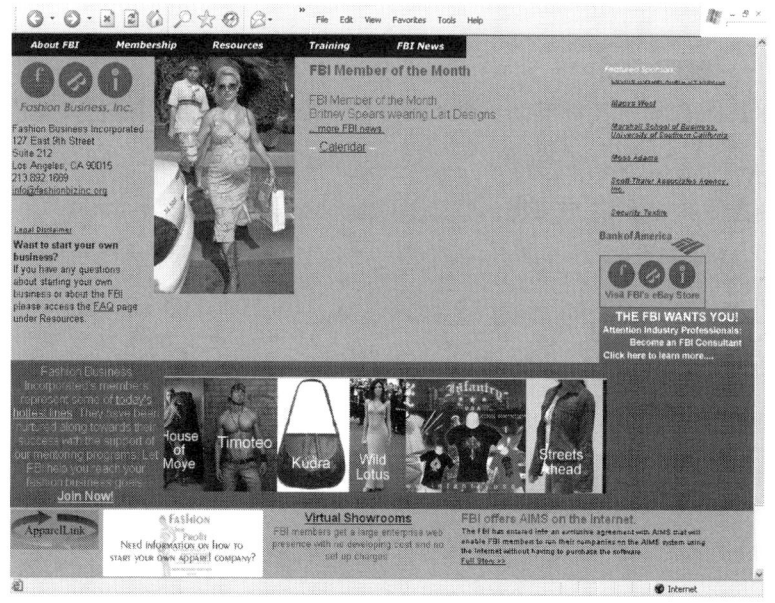

Fashion For Profit By Frances Harder

The Fashion Business is a unique industry: artistic and creative, profit-driven and demanding. **Fashion For Profit** will take you to the heart of the business of fashion and give you the real facts.

A good idea and the right market niche can lead to your ultimate dream of running a successful apparel business. However, it is a multi faceted industry with many important components that should be fully understood before taking that leap of faith. One missing link could mean failure. Knowledge is empowering and could save your savings! **Fashion For Profit** is the book that will support your ideas and help you to realize your dream. You will not only learn what you need to know, but what you want to know.

As you browse this 360-page book you will note that you will get more and more excited. Each chapter brings definitive information about each specific area of apparel manufacturing. You will find that many of the questions you thought would never be addressed anywhere are answered here in clear and understandable terms.

Frances Harder, designer, entrepreneur is also the founder of the LA based FBI (**Fashion Business Inc**.) an educational 501 c (3) non profit which provides much needed business intelligence and support to smaller creative apparel companies. www.Fashionbizinc.org

Title: Fashion For Profit the book
Author: Frances Harder
Published: New revised 6th edition
Contact Information: Harder Publications
3402 Tanglewood Lane,
Rolling Hills Estates,
CA. 90274
Tel: 310 541 7196
Fax: 866 460 7753
www.FashionForProfit.com
email: info@FashionForProfit.com
ISBN # 0-9727763-1-1
Retail: $49.00

Fashion For Profit – DVD
2 hour Seminar Supplement to the book Fashion For Profit

From Design Concept to Apparel Manufacturing….

FA$HION
for
PROFIT

FROM DESIGN CONCEPT TO
APPAREL MANUFACTURING...

A PROFESSIONAL'S COMPLETE GUIDE

2-HOUR SEMINAR SUPPLEMENT
TO THE BOOK FASHION FOR PROFIT

By Frances Harder

The contents of this 2 hour seminar will assist and enlighten you in investigating your market niche, legal and licensing requirements, financial requirements, product development, production, costing, branding and marketing, to ultimately opening your own retail store.

This seminar features: author of Fashion For Profit Frances Harder who is also the founder of the LA based apparel business development center the Fashion Business Incorporated. www.Fashionbizinc.org

Other guests include: Greg Wiseman attorney at law Silver & Freedman, Century City, CA. Pam Roberts PITCH PR & Marketing to the apparel industry, LA. Hanna Hartnell designer/store owner, Santa Monica, CA

Title: Fashion For Profit - 2 hour seminar
Author: Frances Harder
Published: New revised 6th edition
Contact Information: Harder Publications
3402 Tanglewood Lane,
Rolling Hills Estates,
CA. 90274
Tel: 310 541 7196
Fax: 866 460 7753
www.FashionForProfit.com
email: info@FashionForProfit.com
ISBN # 0-9727763-2-X
Retail: $25.00 DVD or VHS available

Fashion For Profit – Forms For Profit
CD - List of forms

Being prepared for doing business in a professional manner means using the correct forms and procedures common in the apparel industry. Forms For Profit will give you the templates, which can incorporate your own logo. These forms will save valuable time in "getting it right"!

Some forms, e.g. invoices, costing sheets, sales order forms have been built in a dynamic format so calculations can be achieved in Microsoft Excel.

Forms For Profit
Blanks plus examples:

§ Sales Order Forms – Blank - plus example
§ Order Confirmation - Blank - plus example
§ Invoice - Blank – plus example
§ Cutting Ticket – Blank – plus example
§ Bill of Materials – Blank -- plus example
§ Pick Ticket – Blank – plus example
§ Purchase Order – Blank – plus example
§ Packing Slips – Blank – plus example
§ Cost Sheets – Blank - plus example

$ Pattern Card – Blank - plus example
$ Specification Sheets – Blank - plus example
$ Sales Rep Agreement
$ Contractors Agreement
$ Credit Check Application
$ Non-Disclosure Agreement

And More…

Also included on this valuable CD are professional body templates that can be used as a base for illustrations, and/or specifications. Print and use, or, use as a guide for Illustrator software for design development – Women's, men's, children's templates.

Retail Price: $19.99

Individual forms are also available for purchase for $5.00 each at www.FashionForProfit.com.

Place
Postage
Here

Harder Publications
3402 Tanglewood Lane,
Rolling Hills Estates,
CA. 90274

Harder Publications Order Form

Phone Orders: (310) 541-7196
Fax Orders: (866) 460-7753
Postal Orders: Harder Publications
3402 Tanglewood Lane, Rolling Hills Estates,CA. 90274
Internet Orders: www.Fashionforprofit.com
Email: info@FashionForProfit.com

Qty	Price*	Item
	@ $19.99 ea	Costing For Profit book
	@ $49.95 ea	Fashion For Profit book
	@ $25.00 ea	Fashion For Profit DVD
	@ $19.99 ea	Forms For Profit CD
	@ $65.00 ea	Fashion For Profit book & DVD
	@ $99.99 ea	Business Starter Package – Costing For Profit, Fashion For Profit, DVD and CD

*Plus tax, shipping and handling

Teaching guide and PowerPoint presentation available for instructional use on college orders.

Sales Tax: Please add 8.25% for products shipped to California addresses.

Shipping: $5 US / $9 International for the first item and $3 for each additional item.

Name: _____

Address: _____

City: _____ State: ___ Zip: _____

Phone:_____ Country: _____

Email Address:_____

Payment Type:
❑ Check enclosed payable to: Harder Publications
❑ Credit Card: ❑ Visa   ❑ MasterCard
Credit card #: _____

Name on card: _____ Exp date: ____

Please send more information on:
❑ Seminars ❑ Consulting ❑ Teaching Material